MW01232656

GERMAN RECIPES FOR EVERYONE

Learn How to lose weight fast while eating the Most Incredible Dutch Recipes, include a detailed process to enjoy food with maximum taste

LINETTE CARROLL

© Copyright 2021 by **TRACY KINSMAN** - All rights reserved.

The following Book is reproduced below with the goal of providing information that is as accurate and reliable as possible. Regardless, purchasing this Book can be seen as consent to the fact that both the publisher and the author of this book are in no way experts on the topics discussed within and that any recommendations or suggestions that are made herein are for entertainment purposes only. Professionals should be consulted as needed prior to undertaking any of the action endorsed herein.

This declaration is deemed fair and valid by both the American Bar Association and the Committee of Publishers Association and is legally binding throughout the United States.

Furthermore, the transmission, duplication, or reproduction of any of the following work including specific information will be considered an illegal act irrespective of if it is done electronically or in print. This extends to creating a secondary or tertiary copy of the work or a recorded copy and is only allowed with the express written consent from the Publisher. All additional right reserved.

The information in the following pages is broadly considered a truthful and accurate account of facts and as such, any inattention, use, or misuse of the information in question by the reader will render any resulting actions solely under their purview. There are no scenarios in which the publisher or the original author of this work can be in any fashion deemed liable for any hardship or damages that may befall them after undertaking information described herein.

Additionally, the information in the following pages is intended only for informational purposes and should thus be thought of as universal. As befitting its nature, it is presented without assurance regarding its prolonged validity or interim quality. Trademarks that are mentioned are done without written consent and can in no way be considered an endorsement from the trademark holder.

TABLE OF CONTENTS

INTRODUCTION 10

SARAZENER (SARACEN) 14

SATARASCH 15

SAUERAMPFERSUPPE 17

(SORREL SOUP)...17

SAUERBRAATEN & POTATO DUMPLINGS 19

SAUERBRATEN 24

(SWEET SOUR BEEF) 24

SAUERBRATEN KLOPSE (SAUERBRATEN MEATBALLS)................26

SAUERBRATEN W/SWEET & SOUR CABBAGE 28

SAUERFLEISCH (BOEUF A LA MODE) 31

SAUERKRAUT SALAD WITH YOGURT DRESSING........................33

SAUERKRAUT SOUP 35

SAUERKRAUTSALAT MIT SCHINKEN (SAUERKRAUT SALAD WITH HAM) 38

SAUERKRAUTSALAT MIT SCHINKEN (SAUERKRAUT SALAD) 40

SAURE KARTOFFEL..42

(SAURE RAEDLE, EINGEMACHTE)...42

SAUREBRATEN & GINGER 44

SCHEITERHAUFEN (LOG PYRE) 47

SCHINKEN ROLLE (HAM LOAF) 49

SCHINKENSPECK > GERMAN BACON 51

SCHLEDDERLES-SUPPE (SCHLETTERSUPPE) 55

SCHLESISCHES HIMMELREICH (SILESIAN PORK)........................57

SCHNECKEN 59

SCHNEIDERFLECKLESUPPE...61

SCHNITTBOHNENSALAT...63

(GREEN-BEAN SALAD)...63

SCHOKOLADENPRETZEL...65

(CHOCOLATE PRETZELS) 65

SCHWAEMME (MUSHROOMS) 68

SCHWALBENNESTER..70

(BARVARIAN VEAL) 70

SCHWEINEKOTELETTS IN SAURER SAHNESOSSE........................72

SCHWEINES MIT BODABIRE AND AEPFEL 74

SCHWEINESCHNITZEL...75

SCHWEINSMEDALLIONS MIT SOMMERMAJORAN 78

SEMMELKRATZET (SEMMELSCHMARREN) 80

SENFGURKEN 81

SPAETZLE NOODLES 83

SPARGEL IN WEISSER SOSSE 85

SPATZLE (SPAETZLE NOODLES) 86

SPECKKARTOFFEL 88

(POTATOES WITH BACON)...88

SPECKKNOEDEL 89

(AUSTRIAN BACON DUMPLINGS) 89

SPECKPFANNEKUCHEN..92

SPECKZELTEN (SPECKPLATZ) 94

CONCLUSION 98

INTRODUCTION

Thank you so much for purchasing this fantastic German recipe book. In this cookbook you will find many recipes of German cuisine, the dishes we are going to make are among the tastiest in all of Germany. German cuisine is extremely varied and innovative, which consists of many ingredients, from fish to shellfish from the North Sea and the Baltic Sea to Bavarian white sausage, as well as endless types of roasts.

For a long time Germany was a set of countries and principalities independent of each other, even from a gastronomic point of view, plus cultural exchanges with neighboring countries have contributed to making this cuisine so varied. I hope that the recipes that I will propose will satisfy your expectations and that you will have fun recreating them.

Enjoy your meal.

Sandtortchen (Sand Tarts)

24 Servings

- 2 1/2 c sugar
- 2 c butter (or margarine)
- 2   eggs, large
- 4 c flour, unbleached, unsifted
  - egg white, large, beaten
- sugar
- cinnamon
- pecan, halves

Cream sugar and butter. Beat in 2 eggs. Gradually blend in the flour. Chill dough overnight. Roll as thin as possible on well-floured board. Work with 1/4 of the dough at a time. Keep remaining dough chilled. Cut into diamonds with a knife. Place on greased cookie sheets.

Brush each cookie with beaten egg white. Sprinkle with sugar and a pinch of cinnamon. Place a pecan half in center of each cookie. Bake in preheated 350-degree F. oven for 8 to 10 minutes or until edges are light brown. Cool on cookie sheets 1 minute, then

remove to wire racks. Store in airtight tins.

Sarazener (Saracen)

<u>4 Servings</u>

- ➢ 600 g liver from European elk or from deer, cut into small
- ➢ 3 1/2 T fat
- ➢ onion, finely chopped
- ➢ 1 T flour
- ➢ 1 T vinegar
- ➢ 4   to 6 cups meat broth

salt and pepper to taste spaetzle

Roast the onions in the fat until golden, then add the liver and sauté it. Add the spices. Stirring constantly, dust liver with flour and then add a little of the broth. Add the remainder of the broth and the spaetzle, and briefly bring once more to a boil. Stir in vinegar to taste.

Satarasch

<u>4 Servings</u>

- ➤ 750 g pork, cubed
- ➤ 5 T vegetable oil
- ➤ 4 md potatoes
- ➤ 2   leeks, cleaned

- red pepper
- green pepper
- md onions
- garlic cloves
- 6   tomatoes, peeled
- salt & pepper
- 1 T paprika
- 1/2 t thyme
- 3/4 l beef stock
- T tomato pure

Peel the potatoes, onion and garlic, clean the leek and peppers and chop them all small. Cube the pork.

Heat the oil in a casserole and fry the pork for about 15 minutes in it. Add the vegetables and the chopped tomatoes. Stir in thyme, salt, pepper and paprika, and pour over the stock. Cover the casserole and simmer for a good hour. Before serving, stir in the

tomato pure and correct seasoning.

Sauerampfersuppe (Sorrel Soup)

4 Servings

- ➢ 1 bn sorrel
- ➢ 1 bn fresh chervil
- ➢ 50 g butter (3 1/2 tbsp)
- ➢ 3 T flour
- ➢ yolk
- ➢ 4 T to 5 tb sour cream
- ➢ 1 1/2 l meat broth (or water
    - ○ -(approx.)
        - - 1 1/2, qts)

A recipe from grandmother's more thrifty times; rarely encountered today.

Melt the butter, and whisk in flour. Add meat broth or water. Add the rinsed and chopped herbs, and briefly bring to a boil. Let soup cool a bit, then thicken with egg yolk. Season with salt, pepper, and a pinch of sugar. Stir in sour cream when serving.

In some Swabian kitchens, very finely chopped garlic gets scattered on top of the soup.

Sauerbraaten & Potato Dumplings

In large saucepan combine 1/2 C dry red wine, 1/2 C red wine vinegar 2 C cold water, a Medium size onion, peeled and thinly sliced, handful of crushed black peppercorns and 4 whole juniper berries (which she crushed in the Pestle, and a couple of bay leaves. Bring this marinade to a boil, then remove from heat and allow to come to room temp.

Place a 5lb boneless top or bottom round roast, with fat trimmed off, in a deep crock just large enough to hold it comfortably.

Pour the cooled marinade over the roast.

Turn the meat to moisten all sides, and covered the crock with the wooden top, and put it out on the porch where it is cold (not freezing), and leave it there for 4-5 days. Everyday turn the meat in the marinade at least two times.

On the 5th day remove the meat from the marinade and completely dried it with towels. Strain the marinade through a fine sieve and reserve the liquid. Throw away the spices in the sieve.

Take a large casserole and melted 3 tbsp lard in it over high heat until it starts to sputter. Add the meat and brown it on all sides and make sure it browns well, without burning.

Take the meat and transfer it to a platter, and pour off and throw away all but a couple of tbsp of the fat from the casserole. Add 1/2 C finely chopped onions, 1/2 C finely chopped carrots, 1/4 C fresh chopped celery to the fat in the casserole and cook over mod. Heat

stirring frequently, for about 6-8 minutes or until they are soft and light brown.

Sprinkle 2 tbsp of flour over the vegies and cook, stirring constantly, for another 2-3 minutes longer, or until the flour begins to color.

Pour 2 C of the reserved marinade and 1/2 C water and bring to a boil over high heat. Return the meat to the casserole. Cover and simmer over low heat for 2 hours or until the meat shows no resistance when pierced with the tip of a sharp knife.

Transfer the meat to a heated platter and cover to keep it warm while making the sauce. Pour the liquid left in the casserole into a large measuring cup and skim the fat from the surface. You will need 2-1/2

Cups of liquid for the sauce. If you have more than that, boil it briskly over high heat until it is reduced to that amount. If you have less, add some of the reserved marinade.

Combine the liquid and 1/2 C crushed gingersnaps or 1 c ready-made honey cake in a small saucepan and cook over mod. heat, stirring frequently for 10 min. The crumbs will disintegrate in the sauce and thicken slightly.

Strain the sauce through a fine sieve, pressing down hard with a wooden spoon to force as much of the vegetables and crumbs through as.

Return the sauce to the pan, taste for seasoning and let it
simmer over low heat till ready to serve.

To serve carve the meat into 1/4" slices and arrange attractively, over lapping layers on a platter. Moisten the slices with a few tbsp of the sauce and pass the remaining sauce separately in a gravy boat.

Sauerbraten
(Sweet Sour Beef)

6 Servings

- 3 1/2 lb. bottom round
- 2 c wine vinegar (heated)
- 2 c water
- 1 1/2 t salt
- 2 T parsley
- 1 t pepper

- ➤ 2 T sugar
- ➤ onion, sliced
- ➤ bay leaf
- ➤ T butter
- ➤ T flour
- ➤ T cold water
- ➤ 1 c beef stock
- ➤ 6   gingersnaps

Heat 2 cups water, and vinegar together until hot. Place meat in crock covered with vinegar and water. [Do NOT use a metal pot!] Add salt, parsley, pepper, sugar, and onion. Cover and refrigerate for 3 days, turning daily. Drain marinade and reserve. Lightly flour meat. Brown well in butter in kettle. Add onion slices and 3 cups marinade. Cover and simmer until tender. Remove meat to a hot serving dish and keep warm. Skim fat off liquid. Mix flour and water and stir into pan, Add stock.

Sauerbraten Klopse (Sauerbraten Meatballs)

<u>4 Servings</u>

- ➢ 1 lb. ground beef, lean
- ➢ 1/4 c milk
- ➢ 1/4 c bread crumbs, dry
- ➢ 1/8 t cloves, ground
- ➢ 1/8 t allspice, ground
- ➢ 1/2 t salt
- ➢ pepper, to taste
- ➢ T vegetable oil
- ➢ 1/2 c vinegar
- ➢ 3/4 t ginger, ground
- ➢ bay leaf
- ➢ T sugar, brown
- ➢ T unbleached flour

Mix beef, milk, crumbs, cloves, allspice, salt and pepper. Form

into meatballs. Brown meatballs in hot oil. Drain off fat. Add 1 cup

water, vinegar, ginger, bay leaf, and brown sugar. Cover and simmer

1/2 hour. Skim off fat. Remove meatballs and keep them warm. Mix

flour and 2 T water. Slowly stir into the pan juices to make gravy.

Pour gravy over meatballs. Serve with buttered noodles.

Sauerbraten W/Sweet & Sour Cabbage

8 Servings

DEIDREANNE PENRODFGGTB

=========

- ➢ 2 c vinegar
- ➢ 2 c water

MARINADE

==========================

- ➢ 1 T salt
- ➢ 1 t cloves
- ➢ 1/2 t thyme
- ➢ 2 t peppercorns
- ➢ 2 T parsley stems
- ➢ 2   bay leaves, small
- ➢ 1/4 c celery leaf, green
- ➢ 2 T garlic, crushed
- ➢ 1/3 c carrots
- ➢ 3/4 c carrots, sliced

- ➢ 1/4 c celery
- ➢ 6 lb. beef, bottom round
- ➢ 1/2 c bacon drippings
- ➢ 1 c red wine
- ➢ 2 c beef stock
- ➢ 1/2 c tomato puree
- ➢ 2 T brown sugar
- ➢ 1/4 c cornstarch

1. Put Water and Vinegar into a stainless-steel stock pot.

2. Add all the Marinate Ingredients.

3. Place Beef in the pot, allowing Marinade to cover the Meat. It should be kept in the refrigerator about 3 to 4 days for pickling, and turned once a day. Remove the Meat from the Marinade, place in a roasting pan with the Bacon Drippings, and sear well on all sides.

4. Place the Marinade and the Wine, Beef Stock, Tomato Puree, and Brown Sugar in a thick-bottomed pot and bring to a boil. Add the seared Meat and simmer for 3 hours, lid on.

5. Reserve Meat in a warm place till ready to carve. Strain the Gravy and reduce to 3 1/2 cups, add diluted Starch, continuously stirring while bringing to a boil. Adjust Seasoning and serve Gravy with carved Meat.

Sauerfleisch (Boeuf A La Mode)

<u>4 Servings</u>

- ➤ 1 Kg beef (shoulder (or leg) (a) generous,2 lbs.)
- ➤ 40 g flour (1/3 cup)
- ➤ 50 g fat (3 1/2 tbsp)
- ➤ onion, finely chopped
- ➤ salt and pepper, To Taste
- ➤ vinegar marinade
- ➤ I water (2 qts plus 1/2 cup)
- ➤ vinegar, To Taste
- ➤ onion
- ➤ a few cloves
- ➤ piece lemon peel
- ➤ 1/2 yellow turnip [substitute carrot]
- ➤ bay leaf
- ➤ a few peppercorns

Colloquially referred to as 'Boefflamott'.

Prepare the marinade by combining all the ingredients and briefly bringing to a boil. After marinade has cooled completely, soak the meat in it for 2 to 3 days. Then remove the meat from the marinade and again bring the marinade to a boil. Add the meat again and cook for 1 1/2 to 2 hours.

Meanwhile, in a large pot, prepare a dark roux of the fat and flour. Add the chopped onion. Gradually add enough hot marinade to obtain a thick gravy. Season to taste with salt, a bit of sugar, and lemon.
Let the cooked, sliced meat briefly steep in the gravy before serving.

Serve with potato dumplings or bread dumplings.

Sauerkraut Salad with Yogurt Dressing

4 Servings

- ➢ 1 lb. sauerkraut, (1 lb. can)
- ➢ 6 oz ham, cooked
- ➢ 1/2 c yogurt
- ➢ 1/4 t pepper, white

Blue grapes dressing ===========

> 1/4 t salt

> 1 t honey

Rinse and drain sauerkraut; chop coarsely. Wash grapes and cut in half; remove seeds if desired. Cut ham in julienne strips. Gently mix these 3 ingredients. Blend dressing ingredients and stir into sauerkraut mixture. Marinate for 10 minutes; adjust seasoning before, if necessary.

Sauerkraut Salad with Yogurt Dressing

<u>4 Servings</u>

- ➢ 1 lb. sauerkraut, (1 lb. can)
- ➢ 6 oz ham, cooked
- ➢ 1/2 c yogurt
- ➢ 1/4 t pepper, white

Blue grapes dressing ===========

> ➤ 1/4 t salt
> ➤ 1 t honey

Rinse and drain sauerkraut; chop coarsely. Wash grapes and cut in half; remove seeds if desired.   Cut ham in julienne strips. Gently mix these 3 ingredients.   Blend dressing ingredients and stir into

sauerkraut mixture. Marinate for 10 minutes; adjust seasoning before, if necessary.

Sauerkraut Soup

<u>1 Serving</u>

- ➤ 1 lg jar sauerkraut
- ➤ 2   apples
- ➤ onion
- ➤ 1 t caraway seed
- ➤ 1/2   head fresh white cabbage
- ➤ smoked pig's knuckle or
- ➤ chunk of ham
- ➤ salt and pepper
- ➤ 1 c apple juice
- ➤ 1 c water
- ➤ garnish
- ➤ sm potatoes, boiled

Simplest recipe for sauerkraut soup: Rinse the s-k, 1 large jar or can, in running cold water. Put in a stainless steel or iron (not aluminum) pot. Chop into chunks 2 apples. Add. Chop 1 onion. Add.

Add 1 teaspoon of caraway seed. Chop 1/2 head of fresh white cabbage. Add. Add 1 smoked pig's knuckle. Salt and pepper to taste. Add 1 cup apple juice(optional) and 1 cup or more water. Simmer covered at least for 45 minutes (time varies, depending on brand of kraut; some is so processed that it may need less time than that!)

Instead of knuckle, uncooked ham chunk may be added. Good, smoked ham would be wasted but not unpalatable. Delicious soup is good if served with boiled, buttered and seasoned potatoes on the side.

If you wish to prepare more soup, for more people than the 2 of you, a whole shoulder can be used with 3 cans or jars of sauerkraut, giving enough meat for everyone. (For a large shoulder to cook thoroughly you would need over an hour of cooking time, if the shoulder had not been precooked. Otherwise, the 30-45 minutes is enough. But you taste and decide!)

Sauerkrautsalat Mit Schinken (Sauerkraut Salad with Ham)

<u>4 Servings</u>

- ➢ 1 lb. sauerkraut, (1 lb. can)
- ➢ 1/2 lb. blue grapes
- ➢ 6 oz ham, cooked

DRESSING

=========================

- ➢ 1/2 c yogurt
- ➢ 1/4 t salt
- ➢ 1/4 t pepper, white
- ➢ 1 t honey

Rinse and drain sauerkraut; chop coarsely. Wash grapes and cut in
half; remove seeds if desired. Cut ham in julienne strips. Gently

If you wish to prepare more soup, for more people than the 2 of you, a whole shoulder can be used with 3 cans or jars of sauerkraut, giving enough meat for everyone. (For a large shoulder to cook thoroughly you would need over an hour of cooking time, if the shoulder had not been precooked. Otherwise, the 30-45 minutes is enough. But you taste and decide!)

Sauerkrautsalat Mit Schinken (Sauerkraut Salad with Ham)

<u>4 Servings</u>

- ➢ 1 lb. sauerkraut, (1 lb. can)
- ➢ 1/2 lb. blue grapes
- ➢ 6 oz ham, cooked

DRESSING

==========================

- ➢ 1/2 c yogurt
- ➢ 1/4 t salt
- ➢ 1/4 t pepper, white
- ➢ 1 t honey

Rinse and drain sauerkraut; chop coarsely. Wash grapes and cut in

half; remove seeds if desired. Cut ham in julienne strips. Gently

mix these 3 ingredients. Blend dressing ingredients and stir into

sauerkraut mixture. Marinate for 10 minutes; adjust seasoning before

serving, if necessary.

Sauerkrautsalat Mit Schinken (Sauerkraut Salad)

<u>4 Servings</u>

- 1 lb. sauerkraut, (1 lb. can)
- 1/2 lb. blue grapes
- 6 oz ham, cooked

DRESSING

==========================

- 1/2 c yogurt
- 1/4 t salt
- 1/4 t pepper, white
- 1 t honey

Rinse and drain sauerkraut; chop coarsely. Wash grapes and cut in
half; remove seeds if desired. Cut ham in julienne strips. Gently

mix these 3 ingredients. Blend dressing ingredients and stir into

sauerkraut mixture. Marinate for 10 minutes; adjust seasoning before serving, if necessary.

Saure Kartoffel

(Saure Raedle, Eingemachte)

<u>4 Servings</u>

- ➤ 500 g new potatoes Boiled (a generous lb.)
- ➤ 80 g butter (or lard (1/3 cup))
- ➤ 1 T flour

- 1/2 l water (2 cups plus 2 tbsp)
- bay leaf
- piece lemon peel
- clove
- onion
- salt and pepper, To Taste
- 1 T vinegar (or), To Taste
- 1 ds caraway seed

Melt the fat and add the finely chopped onion and flour. Sauté until the onion is golden brown. Add the water and all the other seasonings. Cook for 1/2 hour. Strain the sauce and pour it over the hot, sliced potatoes.

Saurebraten & Ginger

<u>10 Servings</u>

- ➢ 4 lb. rump roast, beef, boneless
- ➢ 8   peppercorns
- ➢ bay leaf
- ➢ 1 c water
- ➢ 1/4 c vegetable oil
- ➢ c water, boiling
- ➢ 1/2 c sour cream
- ➢ onions, thinly sliced
- ➢ cloves, whole
- ➢ 1 c white vinegar, mild
- ➢ 1/2 c cider vinegar
- ➢ 1/2 t salt
- ➢ 10   gingersnaps
- ➢ 1 T unbleached flour

Place the beef roast in a deep ceramic or glass bowl. Add onions, peppercorns, cloves, and bay leaf. Pour white vinegar and cider vinegar over the meat; chill, covered, for 4 days. Turn meat twice each day. Remove the meat from the marinade, dry it well with paper towels, and strain the marinade into a bowl. Reserve onions and 1 cup marinade. In a Dutch oven brown the meat on all sides in hot vegetable oil. Sprinkle meat with salt. Pour boiling water around the meat. sprinkle in crushed gingersnaps, and simmer covered for 1 1/2 hours. Turn often. Add 1 cup of reserved marinade and cook meat 2 hours or more, until tender. Remove the meat and keep it warm. Strain the cooking juices into a large saucepan. In a small bowl mix sour cream with flour.

Stir it into the cooking juices and cook, stirring, until sauce is thickened and smooth. Slice meat in 1/4-inch slices; add to hot gravy. Arrange meat on a heated platter and pour extra sauce over it.

Scheiterhaufen (Log Pyre)

4 Servings

- 6 rolls (or an), Sliced equivalent amount of slices
- white [French] bread
- 4 T sugar
- to 4 eggs
- 1 t (heaped) cinnamon
- 125 g raisins and sultanas (4 1/2 oz)
- 1/4 l milk (1 cup plus 1 tbsp)
- 1 ds salt
- 75 g butter (1/3 cup)

Mix the milk, eggs, cinnamon and sugar and beat until smooth. Cut the rolls into quarter inch thick slices, dip into the milk mixture, and then arrange in layers in a buttered baking dish. Scatter raisins and sultanas in between the layers.

Dribble leftover liquid (if any) on top of the sliced rolls, and then dot the top with small dabs of butter.

In order to keep the surface from drying out, cover the top of the dish with aluminum foil. Bake at 350 degrees F for about 30 minutes.

Schinken Rolle (Ham Loaf)

<u>8 Servings</u>

- ➢ 2 c cooked ham --, Chopped
- ➢ 2/3 c bread crumbs
- ➢ 2   eggs
- ➢ 2 T onions, Chopped
- ➢ 2 T parsley, Chopped
- ➢ 2 T celery, Chopped
- ➢ 1/4 t salt

- ➤ 1 c milk
- ➤ 2 T butter --, Melted
- ➤ 3 T catsup

Mix ingredients and place into buttered loaf pan. Bake 30 minutes in 350 F oven. Unmold carefully. Can be served warm or cold.

Schinkenspeck > German Bacon

- for 10 pounds total
- 1/2-gal ice water
- 8 oz kosher salt
- 8 oz Prague powder #1
- 1/2 oz powdered dextrose
- 2 1/2 oz white pepper, Ground
- 1 1/2 oz juniper berries, Ground

It's a lot of work, especially if you're working alone, but it is a beautiful finished product that is well worth the trouble.

The original procedure calls for a whole fresh pork ham, but any I make in the future will be made with pork loins. The reason for that is simple - the center part is round and pork loins are naturally round. If you use a ham, you have to fit together various pieces of

the muscle to get the right shape and use gelatin to hold them together. The loin will make the center more like Canadian bacon, but

that's no problem as far as I'm concerned.

I remove the skin from the bacon before curing. I also spray-pump both the bacon and ham at 10% of their weight with the cure. Then you let them cure for 5 to 6 days at 40 F.

Lay the bacon slab out on a counter top and fit it around the ham. You may have to trim off parts of the ham where it's too wide and fit such trimmings in places where it is too narrow. Just sprinkle them

with unflavored gelatin and they'll stay there after the smoking.

When the bacon fits nicely around the ham, sprinkle it with gelation and tie it up like a rolled rib roast. Working alone, I found skewers helpful for this part of the process, securing one end while I worked

on tying the other. This took nearly an hour on my first attempt!

Then you put the whole thing in a stockinette bag and let it rest in a 135 F smokehouse until it gets to 128 F internal - just like bacon, but it will take longer because of the greater thickness. Mine took about a day. Then you can smoke it, but not too much. I kept mine at

128 F for another day so it would firm up nicely.

It was far too thick for my home slicer, so I took it to the butcher, where I had purchased the meat, and let him cut it on his professional grade slicer (and gave him 4 slices for his trouble). I put it in the freezer first, for about 6 hours, so it was easier to slice consistently.

I found it fried up best at very low heat in a cast iron skillet. The sugar in it will caramelize and make a mess even at moderate temperatures. Then prepare yourself to taste the finest bacon you've ever had - I'm not kidding, the delicacy of the juniper berries and
the faint sweetness makes this a treat you'll never forget.

Schledderles-Suppe (Schlettersuppe)

4 Servings

- ➤ 2 T flour
- ➤ egg
- ➤ salt, To Taste
- ➤ 1 T water
- ➤ soup
- ➤ broth
- ➤ salt
- ➤ nutmeg
- ➤ pepper
- ➤ greens

Combine the first four ingredients in a small beaker-like pot and stir until smooth. (The batter should drip in a long thin thread off the spoon). Tilt the pot and scrape the batter off the edge into the boiling broth. This results in the elongated 'Schletterle' which are sort of halfway between spaetzle and noodles.

Bring to a second boil, and adjust seasoning (salt, nutmeg, pepper, and greens). Serve.

Schlesisches Himmelreich (Silesian Pork)

<u>4 Servings</u>

- ➢ 1 lb. fruit (prunes, Dried apricots, apples, pears)
- ➢ 4 fine pork chops (or 1 lb.)
  - o -Lean
    - pork steaks
- ➢ 2 oz (4 tbsp) lard (or butter)

You will need a medium-sized stewpan with a lid. Soak the fruit for a couple of hours - or overnight if possible - in either plain water or cold tea which will give a darker, richer juice to cover.

Fry the chops in the fat, turning them once, so they take color. Add the fruit and the soaking liquid. Cover and simmer all together for 30 to 35 minutes, or until the fruit is soft and the chops cooked through.

Serve with potato dumplings.

Schnecken

12 Servings

- cottage cheese\oil pastry
- for brushing
- 1 oz (30g) soft butter (or marg.)
- 1/2 oz (70g) raisins (washed and well), Drained
- 1 3/4 oz (50g) almonds (blanched
- filling
- T heaping of sugar
- 1 pk vanillin sugar
- 1 3/4 oz (50g) currants (washed and
- well), Drained
- finely), Chopped
- icing
- 6 oz (170g) icing sugar
- T hot water (approx.)

Roll out the pastry to a rectangle 14x18in. (45x35cm) and brush with the fat. For the Filling: mix together the filling ingredients and distribute evenly over the pastry. Starting from the shorter side, roll up like a swiss roll. Then use a sharp knife to cut off slices

about 1 1/4 in thick. Lay these on a greased baking sheet and flatten slightly.

OVEN: preheat oven for 5 min at very hot (400)

BAKING TIME: 15-20 minutes. For the icing: sieve the icing sugar (powdered sugar) and blend with as much of the water as will five a good coating consistency. Ice the schnecken while still hot.

Schneiderflecklesuppe

<u>4 Servings</u>

- ➢ egg
- ➢ 1 T water
- ➢ salt
- ➢ 200 g flour (1 3/4 cups)
- ➢ meat broth
- ➢ nutmeg, Ground
- ➢ chives

On a pastry board, combine the flour, egg, water and salt into a pasta dough, then roll it out paper thin. Hang the dough over the back of a chair or something similar for drying. After the dough has been drying for 1 1/2 to 2 hours, cut it into 2/3-inch squares. As you spread out the dough on the board, you will have to keep dusting it with flour. Bring some lightly salted water to a boil and cook the

'Fleckle' for about 10 to 15 minutes. Drain, briefly rinse in cold water, and then add to the hot meat broth.   Adjust soup's seasoning,

and top with chopped chives.

Schnittbohnensalat (Green-Bean Salad)

4 Servings

- ➢ 1 lb. green beans, fresh *
- ➢ boiling salted water
- ➢ 1/4 c stock, **
- ➢ T vinegar
- ➢ T vegetable oil
- ➢ 2　onions, med., thinly sliced
- ➢ 1/2 t onions, med

➢ 1 t sugar

*   Green beans should be sliced lengthwise (French Cut). ** Stock

is the water that the green beans were cooked in. (Not regular

 Cook beans in boiling salted water until just tender. Reserve

1/4 cup of the cooking liquid and drain off the rest. Prepare sauce

by combining vinegar, oil, reserved vegetable stock, onions, dill,

and sugar; stir until blended. Pour mixture over beans; marinate

several hours before serving.

Schokoladenpretzel
(Chocolate Pretzels)

<u>8 Servings</u>

- ➢ 1/2 c butter (or margarine)
- ➢ 1/4 c sugar
- ➢ egg, large, beaten
- ➢ 1 t vanilla extract

- 1/4 c milk
- 1/4 c cocoa
- c flour, unbleached, unsifted

COCOA FROSTING

====================

- 2 T cocoa
- 1 1/4 c confectioners' sugar
- 2 T butter (or margarine), melted
- 1/2 t vanilla extract

Cream 1/2 cup butter and the sugar until light and fluffy. Beat in the egg, vanilla, and milk. Sift cocoa and flour. Mix into butter mixture until thoroughly blended. Chill dough until firm enough to handle (about 30 minutes). Using 2 T dough, roll a rope about 12 inches long between your hands. Shape into a pretzel as follows:

Make a loop bout 1 1/2 inches in diameter by crossing the ends, leaving 1-inch tails. Flip the loop down over the crossed ends. Press firmly into place. Place pretzels on greased baking sheets. Bake at

350 degrees F. for about 10 minutes. Make frosting in a small bowl. Mix cocoa and confectioners' sugar. Gradually stir in butter and vanilla. If frosting is too thick, thin with milk. When pretzels are

cool, spread with Cocoa Frosting. Make 2 dozen.

Schwaemme (Mushrooms)

<u>4 Servings</u>

- ➤ 1 Kg mushrooms (king boletes and/or chanterelles)
- ➤ (a generous 2 lbs.)
- ➤ 100 g butter (7 tbsp)
- ➤ 1/2 l water (or beef broth (2cups) plus 2, tbsp)
- ➤ T to 3 tb flour
- ➤ salt and pepper, To Taste
- ➤ 1/8 l cream (1/2 cup plus 1/2 tbsp)
- ➤ bn parsley

a few drops lemon juice

Clean the mushrooms. On larger king boletes, remove the greenish
underneath side of the cap. Cut large mushrooms into 1/6-inch thick

slices. In a wide saucepan, melt the butter, then add mushrooms and

water or broth. The mushrooms will be tender shortly after the

liquid reaches a rolling boil. Stir in the flour paste, and briefly

bring to a boil again. Remove from the heat. Stir in the cream and

chopped parsley, and season to taste. Serve with potato dumplings or

bread dumplings.

Schwalbennester (Barvarian Veal)

<u>4 Servings</u>

- ➤ 1 lb. veal, cut in 4 thin slices
- ➤ 1/2 t salt
- ➤ 1/8 t sugar
- ➤ 1/2 t pepper, white
- ➤ 1 T mustard, Dijon style
- ➤ 4   bacon, slices
- ➤ 4   eggs, large, hard cooked
- ➤ 2 T vegetable oil
- ➤ onion, medium, diced
- ➤ 3/4 c beef bouillon, heated
- ➤ 1 T tomato paste
- ➤ T unbleached flour
- ➤ 1/4 c red wine

Dry veal on paper towels. Roll in a mixture of salt, sugar, white pepper, and mustard. Place a bacon slice on top of each piece of veal. Place an unsliced egg on top of the bacon. Rollup each slice of veal (jelly-roll fashion) and tie together with string. Heat oil

in frypan and brown veal rolls well on all sides. Add onion; sauté for 3 minutes. Add the hot bouillon; cover and simmer gently 25 minutes. Remove the veal from the pan. Remove the strings from the veal and keep veal warm on a serving platter. Add tomato paste too the pan drippings; stir. Thoroughly mix flour and red wine to remove all lumps. Add to sauce and cook until mixture thickens. Add warm veal rolls and heat through. Before serving, place veal rolls on a

platter, pour sauce over the rolls and serve with pureed potatoes.

Schweinekoteletts In Saurer Sahnesosse

<u>6 Servings</u>

- ➢ 6   pork chops
- ➢ garlic clove, minced
- ➢ 1 t caraway seeds, crushed
- ➢ t Hungarian paprika, mild *
- ➢ 1/2 t salt
- ➢ pepper, as desired
- ➢ 1 c white wine, dry
- ➢ 1 c sour cream (optional)

Place the pork chops in an ovenproof casserole. Mix the remaining ingredients, except sour cream, and pour over the chops. Marinate the chops 2 to 3 hours in the refrigerator. Bake the chops, uncovered, in the marinade in a preheated 325-degree F. oven for 1 hour or until tender.

Add more wine if necessary. Stir sour cream into pan juices and heat through but DO NOT boil. Serve chops with sour-cream gravy and buttered noodles or dumplings.

Schweines Mit Bodabire And Aepfel

4 Servings

- 500 g pork (a generous lb.)
- onion
- cloves garlic
- 1/2   yellow turnip [substitute carrot]
- T lard
- 2 T water
- 300 g raw potatoes (approx. 3/4 lb.)
- tart apples

Brown the pork and then cook it to the point of where it is half done. Cut into slices, add the diced potatoes as well as the peeled and diced apples, and stew in its own juices. Add a little water whenever required.

Schweineschnitzel

6 Servings

- ➢ 4 (6-ounce) pork cutlets
- ➢ salt and, Freshly Ground pepper to taste
- ➢ flour for dredging
- ➢ egg
- ➢ 1 t water
- ➢ 1 c fresh bread crumbs
- ➢ 4 T butter (or margarine)

- 1 T capers
- lemon wedges

Pound the cutlets until thin. Sprinkle lightly on both sides with salt and pepper. Dredge them lightly but thoroughly in flour.

Beat the egg lightly with the water and dip the floured cutlets in the mixture; coat with crumbs. Using the side of a kitchen knife, tap the cutlets lightly so the crumbs will adhere well to the meat. Transfer them to a wire rack. Refrigerate for one or two hours. This will help the breading adhere to the cutlets when they are being cooked.

Heat the butter in a large skillet and, when it is hot but not brown or smoking, sauté the cutlets in it until they are golden brown on both sides.

Arrange the cutlets on a heated serving platter and garnish with the capers and lemon wedges. Serve immediately.

Schweinsmedallions Mit Sommermajoran

1 Serving

- 1 1/2 lb. boneless pork loin cutlets (cut no thicker than 1/3 of an inch)
- 1/4 c golden raisins, soaked in white wine
- 1 lg golden delicious apple cored, peeled, quartered,
- 1 lg onion, trimmed, peeled, sliced
- T vegetable oil
- 1/3 c mustard
- 1 c loosely leaves of, Packed
- fresh marjoram, rinsed, chopped
- salt (to taste)
- white pepper, Freshly Ground (to taste)

On a cutting board, season cutlets on both sides with salt and pepper to taste (both optional).

Evenly spread the mustard on only one side of the meat. In a large, covered non-stick pan, over medium heat, heat the oil and sauté onions until lightly golden and limp (about

5-10 minutes). Drain raisins (keep juice). To the translucent onions, add apple slices and raisins. Cook for an additional 5 minutes. Add cutlets, placing them first on the side without the mustard and making space for them by pushing the onions aside. Brown cutlets for about 5-10 minutes on each side. Drizzle the cutlets with raisin wine juice and sprinkle them with the marjoram. Reduce the heat to medium low, cover the pan, and cook the cutlets until they are done.

No pink should be visible when you serve the meat. The internal temperature should be at 160-165 degrees F.

Semmelkratzet (Semmelschmarren)

4 Servings

- ➤ 4   stale rolls thinly, Sliced
- ➤ eggs
- ➤ 1/4 l milk (1 cup plus 1 tbsp)
- ➤ 100 g raisins (3 1/2 oz)
- ➤ 60 g butter (1/4 cup)
- ➤ cinnamon and sugar for dusting

Mix the eggs with the lukewarm milk until smooth and pour over the rolls and raisins. Let the liquid soak in. Then sauté the mixture in plenty of butter and dust with sugar and cinnamon. Serve with stewed apples.

Senfgurken

1 Servings

- ➤ 2 Kg small cucumbers (long as a finger)
- ➤ 6 lg onions, finely diced
- ➤ 3 bn dill, finely chopped
- ➤ 5   bortsch leaves, finely
- ➤ chopped
- ➤ 500 ml white wine vinegar
- ➤ 750 g mustard, medium hot
- ➤ 250 g sugar
- ➤ bay leaves, ground
- ➤ cloves, chopped finely
- ➤ 1 T black pepper, ground

Wash the cucumbers, remove stem, and dry well. Put vinegar, mustard, sugar and the herbs Onions, Dill, Borretsch in a pot and bring to a boil.

Add bay leaves, cloves, and pepper. Bring back to a boil while stirring. Add cucumbers and bring back to boil very carefully. Turn cucumbers occasionally. Fill cucumbers (and cooking juice) in glass jars while very hot and close immediately.

Let cool and store for at least 3 to 4 weeks before using.

Spaetzle Noodles

<u>4 Servings</u>

- ➢ 3 c flour, unbleached
- ➢ 1 t salt
- ➢ 1/4 t nutmeg
- ➢ 4   eggs, large, beaten
- ➢ 1/2 c water, or more
- ➢ 1/4 c butter

Sift flour, salt and nutmeg together in a bowl. Pour eggs and 1/4 cup water into middle of flour mixture, beat with a wooden spoon. Add enough water to make the dough slightly sticky, yet keeping it elastic and stiff. Using a spaetzle machine or a colander with medium holes, press the noodles into a large pot full of boiling salted water.

Cook noodles in the water about 5 minutes or until they rise to the surface. Lift noodles out and drain on paper towels. Brown noodles in melted butter over low heat.

Spargel In Weisser Sosse

4 Servings

- 29 oz white asparagus, (2 cans)
- 2 T margarine
- 2 T unbleached flour
- 1/2 c, asparagus liquid
- 1/2 c milk
- 4 oz ham, cut into julienne strips
- 1/8 t nutmeg, freshly grated
- 1/4 t salt

Drain asparagus spears, reserving 1/2 cup of the liquid. Heat margarine in a saucepan. Add flour; blend. Gradually pour in asparagus liquid and milk. Stir constantly over low heat until sauce

thickens and bubbles. Add cooked ham and seasonings. Gently stir in asparagus spears; heat through but do NOT boil.

Serve in preheated serving dish.

Spatzle (Spaetzle Noodles)

4 Servings

- ➢ 3 c flour, unbleached
- ➢ 1 t salt
- ➢ 1/4 t nutmeg
- ➢ 4   eggs, large, beaten
- ➢ 1/2 c, water, or more
- ➢ 1/4 c butter

Sift flour, salt and nutmeg together in a bowl. Pour eggs and 1/4 cup water into middle of flour mixture, beat with a wooden spoon. Add enough water to make the dough slightly sticky, yet keeping it elastic and stiff. Using a spaetzle machine or a colander with medium holes, press the noodles into a large pot full of boiling salted water.

Cook noodles in the water about 5 minutes or until they rise to the surface. Lift noodles out and drain on paper towels. Brown noodles in melted butter over low heat.

Speckkartoffel
(Potatoes with Bacon)

<u>4 Servings</u>

- ➤ 150 g raw, smoked bacon, finely cubed (about 5 to 6 oz)
- ➤ 500 g potatoes (a generous, Cooked lb.), peeled and cut into mediums slices
- ➤ 1 T lard
- ➤ 4 T to 5 tb sour cream
- ➤ salt, To Taste
- ➤ pepper, To Taste

[In a skillet], melt the lard and briefly fry the onions and bacon. Add the sliced potatoes and sauté until golden brown. Add salt and pepper to taste, and mix in the sour cream.

Speckknoedel
(Austrian Bacon Dumplings)

- ➤ 6 sl slightly stale white bread
- ➤ 5 sl thick cut bacon
- ➤ 1/3 c light cream
- ➤ 1/2 c flour
- ➤ 1/2 t baking powder
- ➤ 1/4 t (heaping) caraway seeds
- ➤ 1/4 t thyme, Dried
- ➤ 1/4 t black pepper, Freshly Ground
- ➤ 1/2 t salt (or), To Taste
- ➤ yolk of one large egg
- ➤ 1 T butter, Unsalted
- ➤ 1/2 c white onions, Sliced
- ➤ 1/2 lb. rinsed and, Drained-sauerkraut
- ➤ 1 T fresh parsley, Chopped

1. Trim the bread slices and cut them into 1/2-inch cubes.

2.   Cut the bacon slices into 1/3-inch squares. Sauté them over moderate heat in a large skillet for about 5 minutes. Stir frequently. Transfer them to paper towels with a slotted spoon, and pat dry.

3. Pour water to a depth of 3 inches into a wide bottomed pot and bring it to a simmer (in preparation for step 8).

4. Brown the bread cubes in the hot bacon fat for 3 to 5 minutes. Transfer them to a large bowl.

5. Add the cream to the bowl. Gently toss the bread until it absorbs all the cream. Add to this mixture the bacon, flour, baking powder, caraway seeds, thyme, pepper, and 1/4 teaspoon of the salt. Beat the egg yolk and add it to the bowl. Gently blend all the ingredients.

6. Shape the mixture into 1 1/4-inch spheres with your hands. (If your mixture is too dry, moisten it with a little more cream.) Place the dumplings on a plate as you make them, arranging them in one layer so they do not touch each other.

7. Melt the butter to moderate heat in a clean large skillet. Add the onions and sauté for 2 minutes. Add the sauerkraut and the remaining salt and blend the mixture. Cover, and cook for 12 minutes.

8. Cook the dumplings in the simmering water for about 10 minutes (start this step as soon as you cover the onion-sauerkraut pan.) You need not turn the dumplings as they will do that by themselves.

9. Transfer the cooked 'speckknoedel' to a warm bowl and cover them
with the onion-sauerkraut mixture. Garnish with parsley and serve
immediately.

Speckpfannekuchen

<u>1 Serving</u>

- ➢ 250 g flour
- ➢ 2   eggs
- ➢ 1/2 l milk
- ➢ salt
- ➢ 150 g bacon
- ➢ fat for frying

Sieve flour into a large bowl. Make a well in the middle. Mix eggs and some milk and pour it in the well. Mix with some of the flour.

Slowly add the remaining milk on stirring well. Season with salt. If there are still lumps in the dough, pour the dough through a fine sieve.

Cut the bacon into very fine slices. Fry the bacon in hot fat until golden-brown. Add the dough and slowly fry the thick pancake golden-brown from both sides. (When baking the first side, cover with a lid.)

Speckzelten (Speckplatz)

<u>4 Servings</u>

- ➤ 500 g flour (4 1/2 cups less 1 tbsp)
- ➤ 1 ds sugar
- ➤ 1/2 t salt
- ➤ 1/4 l milk (1 cup plus 1 tbsp)
- ➤ 10 g yeast (.35 oz)
- ➤ 30 g butter (2 tbsp)
- ➤ topping a
- ➤ 300 g raw smoked bacon, Lean
- ➤ -finely diced, (10 1/2 oz)
- ➤ egg yolk
- ➤ 1 T coriander
- ➤ 1 T caraway seed
- ➤ 1 sm onion, finely chopped
- ➤ salt
- ➤ topping b
- ➤ c cracklings
- ➤ T lard
- ➤ salt

Dough:

In a bowl, mix the flour and salt. Dissolve the yeast and sugar in half the lukewarm milk. Form a well in the flour, and pour the yeast mixture into this well. Dust the liquid with flour, and cover the bowl. Let rest, in a warm spot, for 1/2 hour. Then add the melted
butter and knead and beat the dough until it starts to form small bubbles. Shape into rounds that are about half a finger's width thickness and about 5 inches in diameter. Tweak the edges of the dough into a raised rim. Cover the dough circles with

A) egg yolk and then lightly press in the bacon and add the remainder of the ingredients, OR

B) lard and then lightly press in the cracklings. Season with salt.

Bake at medium heat for 30 minutes. Serve hot.

CONCLUSION

Congratulations on making it to the end of this cookbook. The sweet / savory contrast of German cuisine is much appreciated and meats are often accompanied by fruit-based sauces. It is no coincidence that a dish that has made the Germans famous is the combination of pasta and jam. Germans have a "hatchet" taste and seem to really digest everything: it is not uncommon to see people drinking wine and beer at the same meal and ending the meal with a cappuccino. The portions in German cuisine are often very generous and the vastness of the dishes is incredible. I hope you liked the recipes I proposed you and enjoyed recreating them.

Enjoy.